Double Stop Etudes for the Cello

Book One

by Cassia Harvey

CHP202

©2011 by C. Harvey Publications All Rights Reserved.
6403 N. 6th Street
Philadelphia, PA 19126
www.charveypublications.com

Double Stop Etudes for the Cello, Book One

1

Cassia Harvey

Part One: C Major

©2011 C. Harvey Publications All Rights Reserved.

Double Stop Etudes for the Cello, Book One

2

©2011 C. Harvey Publications All Rights Reserved.

3

Double Stop Etudes for the Cello, Book One

4

Double Stop Etudes for the Cello, Book One

5

Slowly

©2011 C. Harvey Publications All Rights Reserved.

Double Stop Etudes for the Cello, Book One

6

Double Stop Etudes for the Cello, Book One

7

©2011 C. Harvey Publications All Rights Reserved.

Double Stop Etudes for the Cello, Book One

8

9

Part Two: G Major

10

11

Double Stop Etudes for the Cello, Book One

12

13

Double Stop Etudes for the Cello, Book One

14

Double Stop Etudes for the Cello, Book One

15

Double Stop Etudes for the Cello, Book One

16

17

Part Three: F Major

18

Double Stop Etudes for the Cello, Book One

19

©2011 C. Harvey Publications All Rights Reserved.

20

21

Double Stop Etudes for the Cello, Book One

22

©2011 C. Harvey Publications All Rights Reserved.

Double Stop Etudes for the Cello, Book One

23

rit.

Double Stop Etudes for the Cello, Book One

24

25

Part Four: D Major

Double Stop Etudes for the Cello, Book One

26

©2011 C. Harvey Publications All Rights Reserved.

27

28

Part Five: B♭ Major

Double Stop Etudes for the Cello, Book One

29

30

also available from www.charveypublications.com: CHP219

Double Stop Shifting for the Cello, Book One

Cassia Harvey

©2012 C. Harvey Publications All Rights Reserved.

www.ingramcontent.com/pod-product-compliance
Lightning Source LLC
Chambersburg PA
CBHW051430070526
44584CB00023B/3656